KS1
4–6
Years

Master Maths at Home

Extra Challenges

Scan the QR code to help your child's learning at home.

 | **MATHS NO PROBLEM!**

mastermathsathome.com

How to use this book

Maths — No Problem! created **Master Maths at Home** to help children develop fluency in the subject and a rich understanding of core concepts.

Key features of the Master Maths at Home books include:

- Carefully designed lessons that provide structure but also allow flexibility in how they're used. For example, some children may want to write numbers, while others might want to trace.

- Speech bubbles containing content designed to spark diverse conversations, with many discussion points that don't have obvious 'right' or 'wrong' answers.

- Rich illustrations that will guide children to a discussion of shapes and units of measurement, allowing them to make connections to the wider world around them.

- Exercises that allow a flexible approach and can be adapted to suit any child's cognitive or functional ability.

- Clearly laid out pages that encourage children to practise a range of higher-order skills.

- A community of friendly and relatable characters who introduce each lesson and come along as your child progresses through the series.

You can see more guidance on how to use these books at **mastermathsathome.com**.

We're excited to share all the ways you can learn maths!

Copyright © 2022 Maths — No Problem!

Maths — No Problem!
mastermathsathome.com
www.mathsnoproblem.com
hello@mathsnoproblem.com

First published in Great Britain in 2022 by
Dorling Kindersley Limited
One Embassy Gardens, 8 Viaduct Gardens, London SW11 7BW
A Penguin Random House Company

The authorised representative in the EEA is Dorling Kindersley
Verlag GmbH. Arnulfstr. 124, 80636 Munich, Germany

10 9 8 7 6 5 4 3 2 1
001–327068–Jan/22

A CIP catalogue record for this book is available from the British Library.

ISBN: 978-0-24153-909-5
Printed and bound in China

For the curious
www.dk.com

This book was made with Forest Stewardship Council™ certified paper - one small step in DK's commitment to a sustainable future. For more information go to www.dk.com/our-green-pledge

Acknowledgements
The publisher would like to thank the authors and consultants Andy Psarianos, Judy Hornigold, Adam Gifford and Dr Anne Hermanson.

The Castledown typeface has been used with permission from the Colophon Foundry.

Contents

Ruby   Elliott   Amira   Charles   Lulu   Sam   Oak   Holly   Ravi   Emma   Jacob   Hannah

Making and comparing numbers

Starter

Who has the most counters?
Who has the fewest counters?

Example

Compare the number of counters.

Jacob

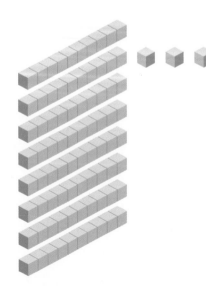

tens	ones
8	3

83 = 8 tens and 3 ones

Emma

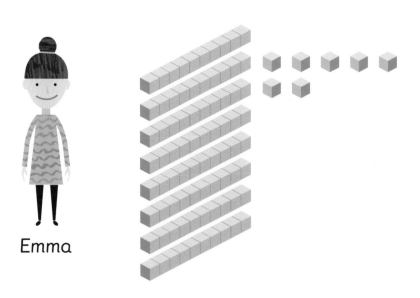

tens	ones
8	7

87 = 8 tens and 7 ones

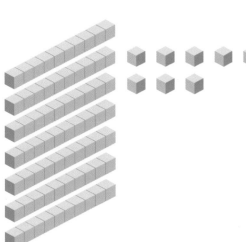

Amira

tens	ones
7	8

78 = 7 tens and 8 ones

Compare the number of tens.

Both 83 and 87 have 8 tens. We compare the ones next.

Emma has the most counters.
Amira has the fewest counters.

We can arrange the numbers from smallest to greatest.

78   83   87

smallest ———→ greatest

1 Use these digit cards to make 2-digit numbers.

| 5 | 7 | 8 |

(a) The greatest 2-digit number I can make is ☐ .

(b) The smallest 2-digit number I can make is ☐ .

(c) Make two more 2-digit numbers. ☐ ☐

(d) Arrange the numbers in order.

☐ , ☐ , ☐ , ☐

smallest   greatest

2 (a) How many 2-digit numbers greater than 20 can be made from the digits 1, 2 and 3?

☐ 2-digit numbers greater than 20 can be made.

(b) Order the numbers you made from greatest to smallest.

☐

greatest   ⟶   smallest

3 Use the number line to fill in the blanks.

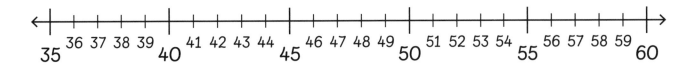

(a)   41   —— 1 more ——→ ☐

(b)   50   —— 1 less ——→ ☐

(c)   47   —— 10 more ——→ ☐

(d)   56   —— 10 less ——→ ☐

(e)   38   —— 20 more ——→ ☐

Completing patterns

Starter

Make two number patterns with the following numbers.
Use each number only once.

| 9 | 15 | 16 | 14 | 12 | 10 |

Pattern 1: ?, ?, 11, ?

Pattern 2: ?, ?, ?, 13

Example

I can put the numbers in order
from smallest to greatest.

| 9 | 10 | ? | 12 | ? | 14 | 15 | 16 |

Pattern 1: 9, 10, 11, 12

Now I can
see a pattern.

2

I can put the numbers in order from greatest to smallest.

| 16 | 15 | 14 | ? | 12 | ? | 10 | 9 |

Pattern 2: 16, 15, 14, 13

Now I can see a pattern.

In pattern 1, the numbers are increasing by 1 each time.
In pattern 2, the numbers are decreasing by 1 each time.

3

We can also make patterns from shapes.

This pattern uses three different shapes.

This is a repeating pattern. ▲●▋ is the part of the pattern that repeats.

1 Complete the number patterns.

(a) 14, 15, ⬚ , ⬚ , ⬚ , 19

(b) 8, ⬚ , 12, ⬚ , 16

(c) ⬚ , 15, 20, ⬚ , 30

(d) 20, ⬚ , ⬚ , 50, 60

2 Find the missing numbers.

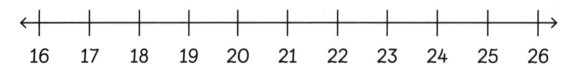

16   17   18   19   20   21   22   23   24   25   26

(a) ⬚ is 1 more than 19.

(b) ⬚ is 1 less than 21.

(c) ⬚ is 2 less than 15.

(d) ⬚ is 2 more than 11.

(e) 25 is ⬚ more than 20.

(f) 10 more than 40 is ⬚ .

(g) ⬚ more than 40 is 42.

(h) 5 less than ⬚ is 35.

3 Complete the number patterns.

(a) 35, 34, 33, 32, 31, [ ] , [ ] , 28

(b) 28, [ ] , 32, 34, 36, [ ] , [ ] , 42

(c) 60, 50, [ ] , 30, [ ] , [ ]

4 (a) Count in fives and shade the boxes in yellow.

1	2	3	4	5	6	7	8	9	10
11	12	13	14	15	16	17	18	19	20
21	22	23	24	25	26	27	28	29	30
31	32	33	34	35	36	37	38	39	40

(b) Count in twos and shade the boxes in blue.

1	2	3	4	5	6	7	8	9	10
11	12	13	14	15	16	17	18	19	20
21	22	23	24	25	26	27	28	29	30
31	32	33	34	35	36	37	38	39	40

5 Holly uses this picture to make a pattern:

Draw the missing piece of the pattern.

6 Continue the patterns by drawing two more shapes.

(a)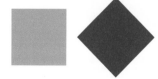

(b)

(c)

7 Fill in the missing shape in this pattern.

8 Draw a repeating pattern from ▽ ▲ ●.

Show three repeats of the pattern.

9 Draw your own repeating pattern using shapes and colours.
Show three repeats of the pattern.

Adding and subtracting

Starter

There are 13 ladybirds on a branch. 5 more come to join them.
How many ladybirds are there altogether?

Example

There are 13 ladybirds on the branch.

I can see 5 ladybirds flying.

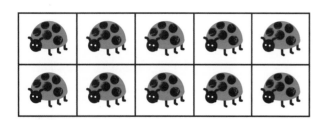

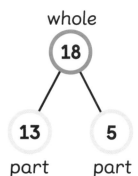

whole

18

13   5

part   part

There are 18 ladybirds altogether.

14

1

How many candles are there altogether?

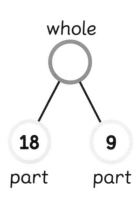

whole

18   9

part   part

There are candles altogether.

2 bakes 12 vanilla cookies and 18 chocolate cookies.

How many cookies does she bake in total?

part

whole

part

 bakes cookies in total.

3 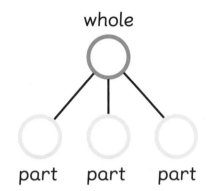 is reading a book. He reads 8 pages on Monday, 7 pages on Tuesday and 9 pages on Wednesday. How many pages does he read altogether?

whole

part   part   part

reads ⬜ pages altogether.

4

Lulu needs to place 11 of the flowers in a vase.
How many flowers will be left?

whole

part   part

⬜ flowers will be left.

5 There are 17 books on a bookshelf.
Emma takes 9 books.
How many books are left on
the bookshelf?

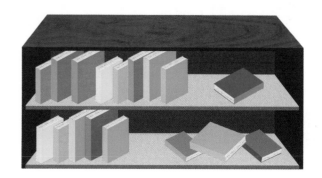

There are ⬚ books left on the bookshelf.

6 Charles has 21 stickers.
He gives 2 to Holly and 3 to Ruby.
How many stickers does Charles have left?

Charles has ⬚ stickers left.

Families of addition and subtraction facts

Starter

 uses 6 , 4 and 2 to make addition and subtraction equations.

How many can she make?

Example

$2 + 4 = 6$

$4 + 2 = 6$

$6 - 4 = 2$

$6 - 2 = 4$

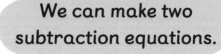
We can make two addition equations.

We can make two subtraction equations.

This is a family of addition and subtraction facts.

Does it matter in what order we add the numbers?

 can make 4 addition and subtraction equations.

1 Use 15, 5 and 20 to make a family of addition and subtraction facts.

☐ + ☐ = ☐   ☐ − ☐ = ☐

☐ + ☐ = ☐   ☐ − ☐ = ☐

2

$$\triangle + 5 = 9$$

Make a family of addition and subtraction facts.

△ + 5 = 9   9 − △ = 5

☐ + ☐ = ☐   ☐ − ☐ = ☐

△ is ☐ .

3 Use these numbers to make a family of addition and subtraction facts.

| 11 | 3 | 8 |

☐ + ☐ = ☐   ☐ − ☐ = ☐

☐ + ☐ = ☐   ☐ − ☐ = ☐

Adding by counting on

Starter

I have 11 counters in this hand. I have 23 counters in total.

How many counters are in Holly's bag? How can you find out?

Example

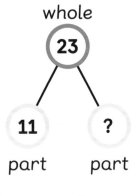

whole

23

11   ?

part   part

23 = 11 + ?

What do I add to 11 to make 23?

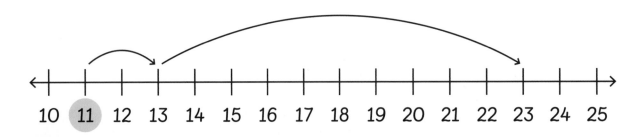

10 11 12 13 14 15 16 17 18 19 20 21 22 23 24 25

23 = 11 + 12

whole

(12)

2   10

part   part

whole

(23)

11   12

part   part

There are 12 counters in Holly's bag.

Practice

1 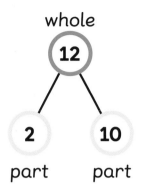 has £7 and she needs £20 to buy a 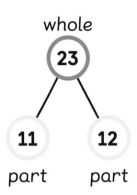.

How much more money does she need?

part

◯

whole

(20)

part

7

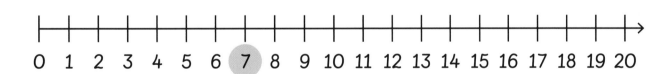

0 1 2 3 4 5 6 7 8 9 10 11 12 13 14 15 16 17 18 19 20

 needs £ ☐ more to buy the .

2 has to read 20 pages of his book by Friday. So far he has read 13 pages. How many more pages must he read?

Do we need to add or subtract?

 must read ☐ more pages.

3 Ravi has 18 football cards.
He needs 25 football cards to complete the set.
How many more football cards does Ravi need?

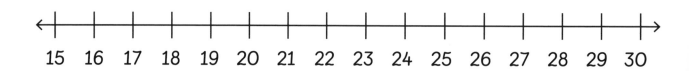

15 16 17 18 19 20 21 22 23 24 25 26 27 28 29 30

Ravi needs ☐ more football cards.

4 Class 1 have put 19 chairs out in the school hall.
They need to put 32 chairs out altogether.
How many more chairs do they need to put out?

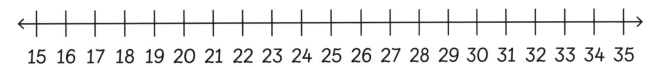

15 16 17 18 19 20 21 22 23 24 25 26 27 28 29 30 31 32 33 34 35

Class 1 need to put out ☐ more chairs.

5 Emma has 40 seeds. She plants 23 seeds.
How many more seeds does she have left to plant?

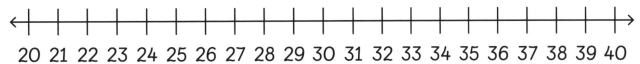

20 21 22 23 24 25 26 27 28 29 30 31 32 33 34 35 36 37 38 39 40

Emma has ☐ more seeds left to plant.

Solving word problems

Starter

Elliott has 9 crayons.
Ruby gives him 8 more crayons.
How many crayons does Elliott have now?

Example

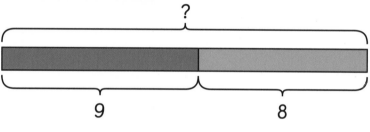

$9 + 8 = 10 + 7 = 17$

1   7

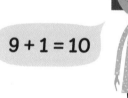

$9 + 1 = 10$

$9 + 8 = 17$
Elliott has 17 crayons.

Practice

1 has 19 toys. has 7 toys.

(a) How many toys do and have altogether?

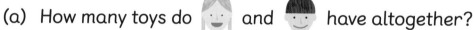

 and have [ ] toys altogether.

(b) Write your own word problem using 19 and 7.

There are 19 [ ] and 7 [ ] .

How many [ ] are there altogether?

2 [face] has a watering can filled with 15 l of water. He uses 6 l of water to water his plants. How much water is left in the watering can?

[ ]

[bar model] ? [ ]

[ ] l of water is left in the watering can.

3 There are 32 cherries in a bowl. [face] eats 8 of them. How many cherries are left?

[ ]

[bar model] [ ] ?

[ ] cherries are left.

4 [face] is saving some money. He has saved £5 and needs £25 to buy a game. How much more money does he need to save?

[face] needs to save £ [ ] .

Solving more word problems

Starter

 has 17 stamps.

 has 5 more stamps than has.

How many stamps does have?

Example

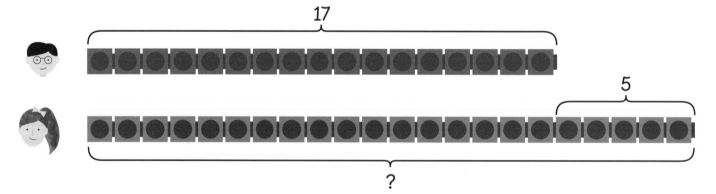

$17 + 5 = 22$

 has 22 stamps.

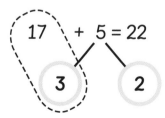

26

1 Elliott makes 14 fruit lollies.
Emma makes 6 more fruit lollies than Elliott makes.
What is the total number of lollies that Emma makes?

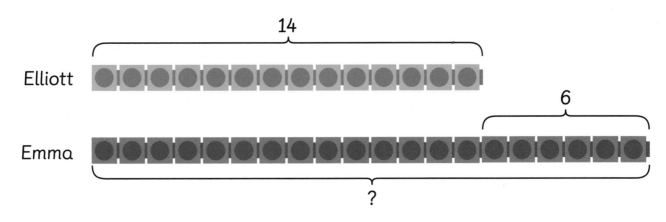

Emma makes ⬜ fruit lollies.

2 Holly has 12 marbles.

Amira has 5 fewer marbles than Holly has.
Charles has 3 more marbles than Holly has.

(a) Draw this information on the picture below.

(b) [　　　　] has the most marbles.

(c) [　　　　] has the fewest marbles.

(d) Charles has [　　] more marbles than Amira has.

(e) Together Holly and Amira have [　　] marbles.

3 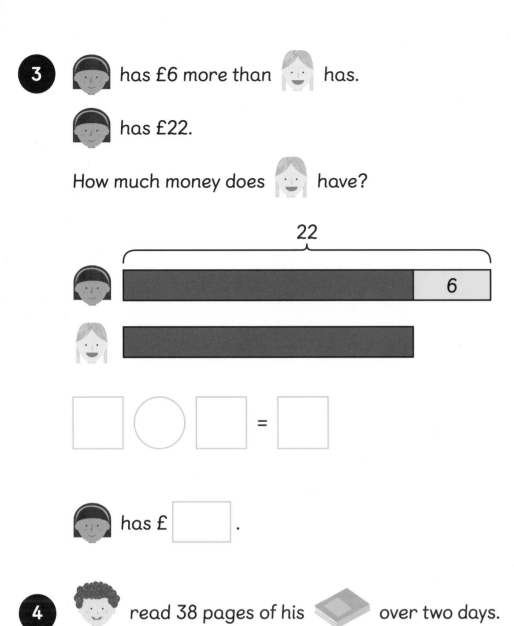 has £6 more than has.

has £22.

How much money does have?

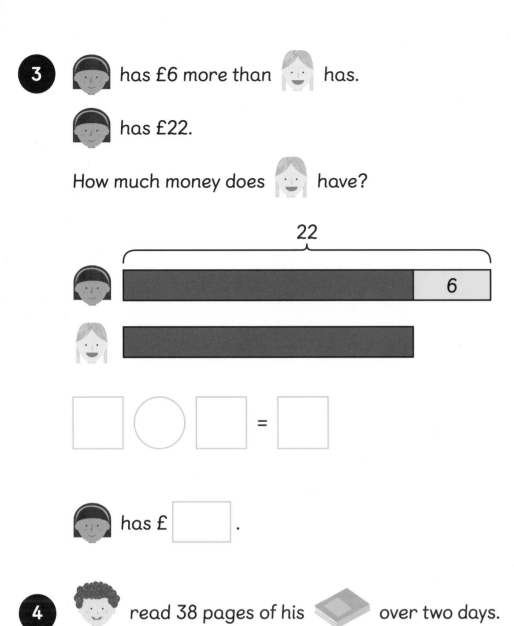

□ ○ □ = □

has £ □ .

4 read 38 pages of his over two days.

On the second day, he read 11 pages.
How many pages did he read on the first day?

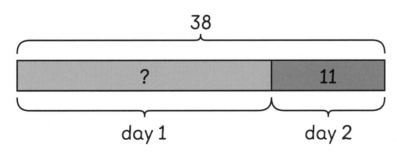

read □ pages on the first day.

5   Make a subtraction problem with the numbers 10 and 6.

What words do you need to use?

Left, fewer, less, take away?

6   Use the numbers 14 and 20 to make two different word problems. Make one addition problem and one subtraction problem.

7   The answer to a word problem is 9. What could the word problem be?

(a)   Can you make an addition problem with the answer 9?

(b)   Can you make a subtraction problem with the answer 9?

8 Make some word problems using this picture.

What are the children doing?

Making equal groups

 has 15 plums.

She puts an equal amount of plums into each bowl.

How many plums are in each bowl?

Example

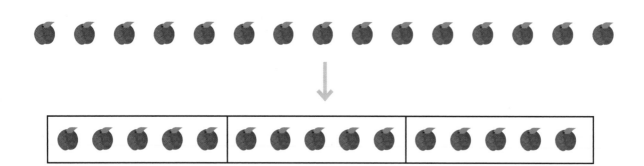

There are [ ] plums in each bowl.

Put 15 plums into 3 equal groups.

1

Move the pencils so that there is an equal amount of pencils in each cup.

(a) How many pencils are in each cup?

There are ⬚ pencils in each cup.

(b) If there are 4 cups and the same number of pencils, how many pencils will be in each cup?

There will be ⬚ pencils in each cup.

2

(a) Put the stars into groups of 5. How many groups are there?

There are ⬚ groups of 5 stars.

(b) Put the stars into groups of 4. How many groups are there?

There are ⬚ groups of 4 stars.

3

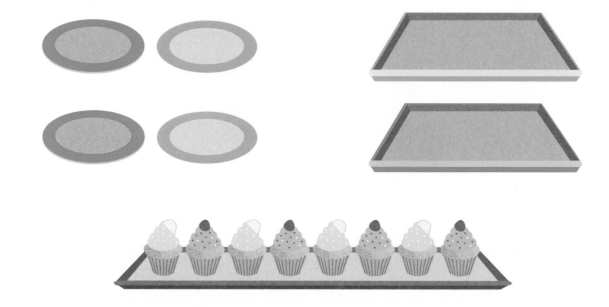

Look at this picture with a member of your family.
Can you think of a word problem for this picture?
What questions can we ask?

4 Put 20 equally into 4 bowls.

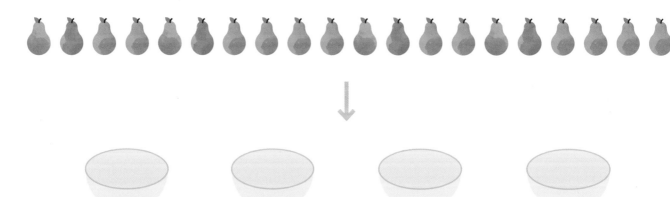

There are [ ] in each bowl.

5 Hannah puts 25 pens equally into 5 pencil cases.

How many pens are in each pencil case?

There are [ ] pens in each pencil case.

Adding equal groups

Starter

There are 2 sandwiches in each lunchbox.
How many sandwiches are in 3 lunchboxes?

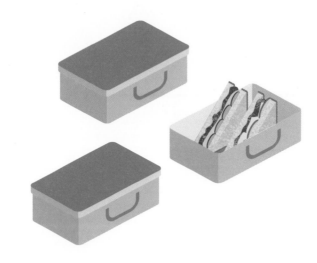

Example

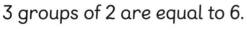

2, 4, 6

3 groups of 2 are equal to 6.
3 twos = 6

There are 6 sandwiches in 3 lunchboxes.

1 There are 10 doughnuts in one box.
How many doughnuts are in 4 boxes?

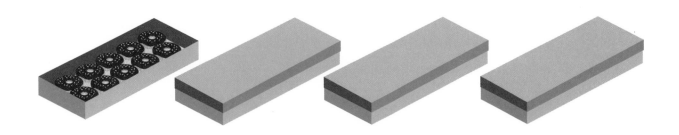

4 groups of ☐ are equal to ☐ .

There are ☐ doughnuts in 4 boxes.

2 There are 5 marbles in each bag.
How many marbles are in 7 bags?

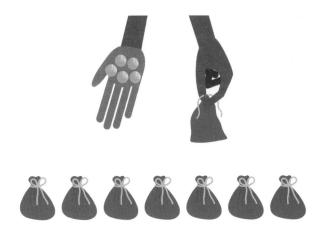

7 groups of ☐ are equal to ☐ .

There are ☐ marbles in 7 bags.

Sharing and grouping

Starter

Holly puts 1 quarter of the tennis balls into a basket.
How many tennis balls are in the basket?

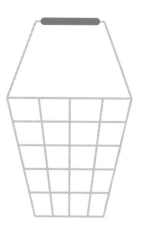

Example

1 quarter	1 quarter

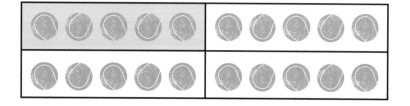

1 quarter	1 quarter

Divide the whole amount into 4 equal parts.

1 quarter of 20 tennis balls is 5 tennis balls.
There are 5 tennis balls in the basket.

1 There are 16 eggs. Holly takes half of them.
Elliott takes a quarter of them.

16

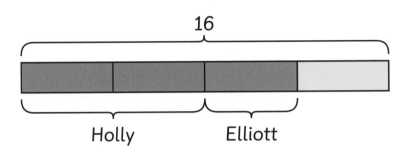

Holly   Elliott

How many eggs does each child take?

Holly takes ☐ eggs.

Elliott takes ☐ eggs.

2 Ravi gives 1 quarter of his 24 cards
to Charles.
How many cards does he give
to Charles?

Ravi gives ☐ of his cards to Charles.

3 There are 8 biscuits in a box. Emma takes 1 quarter of
the biscuits. How many biscuits does Emma take?

Emma takes ☐ biscuits.

Measuring length and height

Starter

Compare the lengths of the objects.

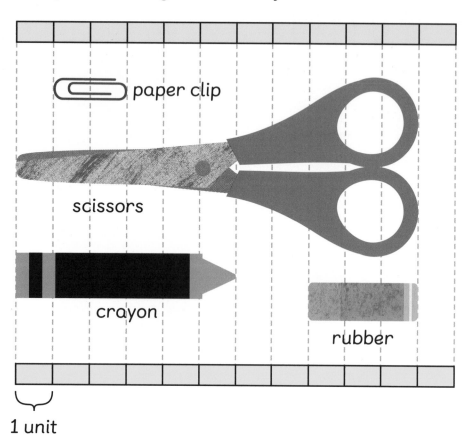

1 unit

Example

1. The ✂ are the longest. They are 11 units long.

   The ▭ is the shortest. It is 2 units long.

   The ▬ is longer than the ▭ and shorter than the ▬.

2

Holly measures the length of a table using a book.

The table is 5 long.

Holly measures the height of a table using a book.

The table is 4 tall.

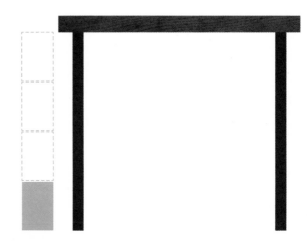

Practice

1 Use a book to measure these items.

Item	Height	Length
sofa		
bed		
table		

2 Measure these lines with a ruler.

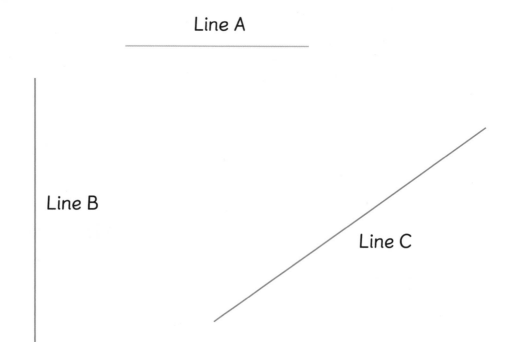

Line A

Line B

Line C

Record your answers here.

Line	Length (cm)
Line A	
Line B	
Line C	

Use **longer** or **shorter** to fill the blanks.

(a)   Line A is ⬚ than Line B.

(b)   Line B is ⬚ than Line C.

(c)   Line C is ⬚ than Line A.

3 Use a ruler to measure the sides of this shape.
Fill in the blanks.

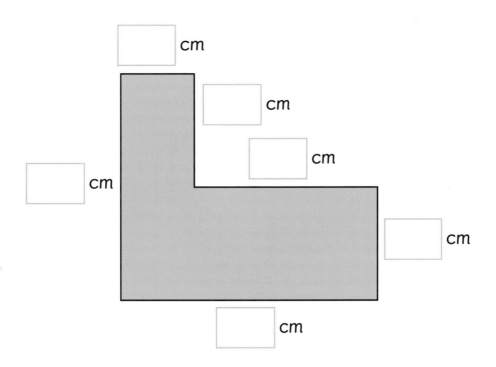

4 Use a ruler to draw lines with the following lengths:

(a) 9 cm

(b) 12 cm

Identifying shapes

Holly drew a building using different shapes.
What shapes has she used to draw the building?

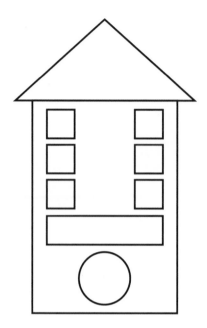

Holly used these shapes.

Name of shape		Number of shapes
□	square	6
▭	rectangle	2
△	triangle	1
○	circle	1

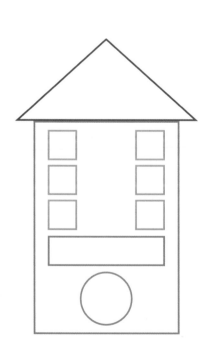

Look at this picture.

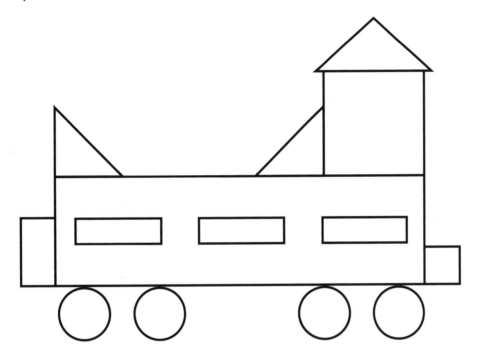

How many of each shape can you find?

Name of shape	Number of shapes
☐ square	
▭ rectangle	
◺ triangle	
○ circle	

Answers

Page 6   **1 (a)** The greatest 2-digit number I can make is 87. **(b)** The smallest 2-digit number I can make is 57. **(c)** Any two of: 58, 75, 78, 85 **(d)** 57, then any 2 of: 58, 75, 78, 85, 87
2 (a) 6 2-digit numbers greater than 20 can be made. **(b)** 33, 32, 31, 23, 22, 21

Page 7   **3 (b)** 42 **(b)** 49 **(c)** 57 **(d)** 46 **(e)** 58

Page 10   **1 (a)** 16, 17, 18 **(b)** 10, 14 **(c)** 10, 25 **(d)** 30, 40   **2 (a)** 20 is 1 more than 19. **(b)** 20 is 1 less than 21. **(c)** 13 is 2 less than 15. **(d)** 13 is 2 more than 11. **(e)** 25 is 5 more than 20. **(f)** 10 more than 40 is 50. **(g)** 2 more than 40 is 42. **(h)** 5 less than 40 is 35.

Page 11   **3 (a)** 30, 29 **(b)** 30, 38, 40 **(c)** 40, 20, 10

4 (a)

1	2	3	4	5	6	7	8	9	10
11	12	13	14	15	16	17	18	19	20
21	22	23	24	25	26	27	28	29	30
31	32	33	34	35	36	37	38	39	40

(b)

1	2	3	4	5	6	7	8	9	10
11	12	13	14	15	16	17	18	19	20
21	22	23	24	25	26	27	28	29	30
31	32	33	34	35	36	37	38	39	40

Page 12   **5** **6 (a)** **(b)** **(c)**

Page 13   **7** ⬤ **8-9** Answers will vary.

Page 15   **1** There are 27 candles altogether.   **2** Emma bakes 30 cookies in total.

Page 16   **3** Jacob reads 24 pages altogether.   **4** 19 flowers will be left.

Page 17   **5** There are 8 books left on the bookshelf. **6** Charles has 16 stickers left.

Page 19   **4** 15 + 5 = 20, 5 + 15 = 20, 20 − 15 = 5, 20 − 5 = 15   **2** 4 + 5 = 9, 9 − 4 = 5, is 4. **3** 8 + 3 = 11, 3 + 8 = 11, 11 − 8 = 3, 11 − 3 = 8

Page 21   **1** Ruby needs £13 more.

Page 22   **2** Sam must read 7 more pages. **3** Ravi needs 7 more football cards.

Page 23   **4** Class 1 need to put out 13 more chairs. **5** Emma has 17 more seeds left to plant.

Page 24   **1 (a)** Hannah and Emma have 26 toys altogether.

Page 25   **(b)** Answers will vary. **2** 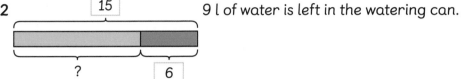   9 l of water is left in the watering can.

3 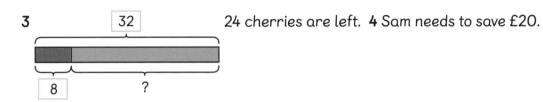   24 cherries are left. **4** Sam needs to save £20.

Page 27   **1** 14 + 6 = 20, Emma makes 20 fruit lollies.

Page 28   **2 (a)** Amira has 7 marbles, Charles has 15 marbles. **(b)** Charles has the most marbles.
  (c) Amira has the fewest marbles. **(d)** Charles has 8 more marbles than Amira has.
  (e) Together Holly and Amira have 19 marbles.

Page 29   **3** 22 − 6 = 16, Hannah has £16. **4** Elliott read 27 pages on the first day.

Page 30   **5–7** Answers will vary.

Page 31   **8** Answers will vary.

Page 33   **1 (a)** There are 4 pencils in each cup. **(b)** There will be 3 pencils in each cup.
  2 (a) There are 4 groups of 5 stars. **(b)** There are 5 groups of 4 stars.

Page 34   **3** Answers will vary. **4** There are 5 pears in each bowl.

Page 35   **5** There are 5 pens in each pencil case.

Page 37   **1** 4 groups of 10 are equal to 40. There are 40 doughnuts in 4 boxes.
  2 7 groups of 5 are equal to 35. There are 35 marbles in 7 bags.

Page 39   **1** Holly takes 8 eggs, Elliott takes 4 eggs. **2** Ravi gives 6 of his cards to Charles.
  3 Emma takes 2 biscuits.

Page 41   **1** Answers will vary.

Page 42   **2** Line A 5 cm, Line B 7 cm, Line C 9 cm **(a)** Line A is shorter than Line B. **(b)** Line B is
shorter than Line C. **(c)** Line C is longer than Line A.

Answers continued

Page 43   **3**

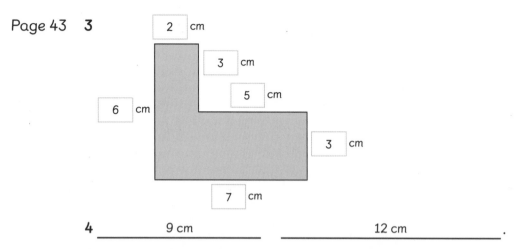

4 ___9 cm___ ___12 cm___ .

Page 45   2 squares, 5 rectangles, 3 triangles, 4 circles.